A 30-DAY DEVOTIONAL TREASURY

GEORGE MÜLLER

Faith

COMPILED AND EDITED BY

LANCE WUBBELS

Emerald Books

P.O. Box 635
Lynnwood, WA 98046

Emerald Books are distributed through YWAM Publishing. For a full list of titles, including other devotionals and classics, visit our website at www.ywampublishing.com or call 1-800-922-2143.

30-Day Devotional Treasuries Series

Introduction

George Müller (1805–1898) has been called the "apostle of faith," and the narrative of God's dealing with him has been termed "the life of trust." He spent more than seventy years of his long life in one grand, unceasing endeavor to proclaim Christ and glorify His name among men. It was the supreme, the all-consuming devotion of his heart. He came to be considered the mightiest person spiritually of his age. A being whose every fiber was bound up in God. A man whose example of faith and prayer will ever remain as one of the brightest possessions of the church on earth.

Though confirmed in the church at the age of fourteen, Müller was raised without a real concept of God. By the time he was sixteen, he was in jail as a vagabond and thief. In his early twenties he came in contact with a group of people who met regularly for prayer and Bible study. Through their witness he was brought to a turning point in his life and was born into the family of God.

In 1834 Müller formed "The Scriptural Knowledge Institution for Home and Abroad," to stimulate education "upon scriptural principles," to circulate Bibles, and to help missionary work. The largest ministry to come out of this work was the numerous orphanages he built and operated on Ashley Down in Bristol, England. He opened his first orphanage for thirty children in April 1836. From the beginning he renounced a regular salary and refused throughout the rest of his life to make any requests for financial support either for himself or for his philanthropic projects, even though sometimes he was penniless. During the next sixty-three years, Müller received nearly one and a half million pounds in answer to prayer, and the many branches of his work included the care of some ten thousand children.

George Müller learned the secret of boldly coming to the throne of God to receive all his needs.

Having experienced God himself, he realized that the puny supplies of man were dwarfed beside the reservoirs of God's grace which he tapped by faith. He learned to not bind God by the limits of his own faith, and for seventy-three years he never found the throne vacant nor the supplies exhausted. He kept asking, knowing that God, who heard, was able to answer.

Triumphant Faith

———✴———

"Don't be afraid; just believe."
—MARK 5:36

As long as we are able to trust in God, holding fast in our heart that He is able and willing to help those who rest on the Lord Jesus Christ for salvation and in all matters that are for His glory and their good, the heart remains calm and peaceful. It is only when we *practically* let go of faith in His power or His love that we lose our peace and become troubled. Remember that it is the very time for *faith* to work when *sight* ceases. The greater the difficulties, the easier for faith. As long as there remains certain natural prospects for help, faith does not rise up as easily as when all natural prospects fail.

All children of God, whatever their position in the world or in the church, should put their trust in God for everything connected with their body, their soul, their business, their family, their church position, their service for God, etc. And it is impossible to do so without enjoying the blessedness that results from it. First comes the peace of God that keeps the heart and mind like a garrison, and second comes a true liberty with regard to circumstances, times, places, and people.

> *As long as there remains certain natural prospects for help, faith does not rise up as easily as when all natural prospects fail.*

Faith is above circumstances. No war, no fire, no water, no business panic, no loss of friends, no death can touch it. It goes on its own steady course. It triumphs over all difficulties. It works most easily in the greatest difficulties. Those who really confide in God, because they know the power of His arm and the love of His heart as demonstrated in the death and resurrection of His only begotten Son, are helped, whatever their trials and difficulties might be.

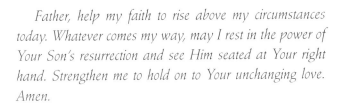

Father, help my faith to rise above my circumstances today. Whatever comes my way, may I rest in the power of Your Son's resurrection and see Him seated at Your right hand. Strengthen me to hold on to Your unchanging love. Amen.

Persevering Faith

———∽∽∽———

And without faith it is impossible to please God,
because anyone who comes to him must believe that he exists
and that he rewards those who earnestly seek him.
—HEBREWS 11:6

Take all of your temporal and spiritual needs to the Lord in prayer. Bring also the necessities of your friends and relatives to the Lord. Only bring your request, and you will perceive how able and willing He is to help you. If you do not immediately obtain answers to your prayers, do not be discouraged, but continue patiently, believingly, perseveringly to wait upon God. Just as surely as that which you ask would be for your real good, and therefore for the honor of the Lord, and as assuredly as you ask it solely on the grounds of the worthiness of our Lord Jesus, so assuredly you will at last obtain the blessing. I myself have had to wait upon God concerning certain matters for years before I obtained answers to my prayers, but at last they came…. The great point is that we ask only for what will bring glory to God; for that, and that alone, can be for our real good.

The great point is that we ask only for what will bring glory to God; for that, and that alone, can be for our real good.

But it is not enough that the thing for which we ask God be for His honor and glory, but we must ask it in the name of the Lord Jesus, expecting it only on the grounds of His merits and worthiness. We must also believe that God is able and willing to give us what we ask from Him. Then we should continue in prayer until the blessing is granted, without fixing a time when, or the circumstances under which, God should give the answer. Patience should be constantly exercised in connection with our prayer. We should, at the same time, look out for and expect an answer until it comes. If we pray in this way, we shall not only have answers, thousands of answers to our prayers, but our own souls will be greatly refreshed and invigorated in connection with these answers.

———∞∞∞———

Heavenly Father, I believe in You with all my heart and soul, and I bring my requests to You in the name of Jesus. You are able to do exceeding abundantly beyond anything I can ask or think. I wait upon You now for the answers I seek. Help me to be patient and unshakable in my faith. Amen.

Increasing Faith

———✦———

The apostles said to the Lord,
"Increase our faith!"
—LUKE 17:5

I n order to have our faith *strengthened,* we must remember that "every good and perfect gift is from above, coming down from the Father of the heavenly lights, who does not change like shifting shadows" (James 1:17). As the increase of faith is a good gift, it must come from God, and therefore He should be asked for this blessing.

The following means, however, should be used for the increase of faith: the careful, diligent reading of the Word or God, combined with meditation on it. Through reading His Word, and especially through meditation on it, the believer becomes increasingly acquainted with the nature and character of God, and thus sees more and more, besides that He is just and holy, what a kind, loving, gracious, merciful, mighty, wise, and faithful Being He is. Thus in times of poverty, affliction of body, bereavement in his family, difficulty in his service, or need of housing or employment, he will rest upon the *ability* of God to help him, because he has not only learned from His Word that He is of almighty power and infinite wisdom, but he has also seen instance upon instance in the Scriptures in which God's almighty power and infinite wisdom have been *actually exercised* in helping and delivering His people. The believer will rest upon the *willingness* of God to help him, because he has not only learned from the Scriptures what a kind, good, merciful, gracious, and

> *Through reading His Word, and especially through meditation on it, the believer becomes increasingly acquainted with the nature and character of God.*

faithful Being God is, but because he has also seen in the Word of God how, in a great variety of instances, He has *proved* Himself to be so. Thus, the reading of the Scriptures combined with meditation of them will be one special means to strengthen our faith.

———

Father, there are no shortages of biblical proofs of Your wonderful character and trustworthiness. Strengthen me with power through Your Spirit in my inner being, so that Jesus may dwell in my heart through faith. Establish me in Your love and give me the power to grasp how wide and long and high and deep Your love is, O Jesus of Nazareth. Amen.

A Pure Heart

━━━∞∞∞━━━

If I had cherished sin in my heart,
the Lord would not have listened;
but God has surely listened
and heard my voice in prayer.
—PSALM 66:18–19

It is of utmost importance that we seek to maintain an upright heart and a good conscience, and therefore do not knowingly and habitually indulge in those things that are contrary to the mind of God. This is particularly the case with reference to *growth in faith*. All my confidence in God, all my leaning upon Him in the hour of trial will be gone if I have a guilty conscience and do not seek to put away this guilty conscience, but still continue to do things that are contrary to His mind. And if in any particular

instance I cannot trust in God because of my guilty
conscience, then my faith is weakened by that
instance of distrust; for faith with every fresh trial of
it either increases by trusting God
or decreases by not trusting Him.
Consequently, there is less and
less power of looking simply and
directly to Him, and a habit of
self-independence is begotten and
encouraged. Either we trust in
God, and in that case we neither
trust in ourselves, nor in our fellow men, nor in circumstances,
nor in anything beside; or we *do* trust in one or more
of these, and in that case do *not* trust in God.

*Faith with
every fresh
trial of it either
increases by
trusting God
or decreases by
not trusting Him.*

Remember that when God orders something to
be done for the glory of His name, He is both able
and willing to find the needed individuals for the
work and the means required. Thus, when the
Tabernacle in the Wilderness was to be erected, He
not only equipped individuals for the work, but He
also touched the hearts of the Israelites to bring the
necessary materials and gold, silver, and precious

stones. All these things were not only brought, but in such abundance that a proclamation had to be made in the camp that no more articles should be brought, because there were more than enough. And again, when God for the praise of His name would have the Temple to be built by Solomon, He provided such an amount of gold, silver, precious stones, brass, iron, etc. for it, that all the palaces and temples that have been built since have been most insignificant in comparison.

<hr />

Search me, O God, and know my heart; test me and know my anxious thoughts. See if there is any offensive way in me, and lead me in the way everlasting. Amen.

Solely Rest in God

—◦◦◦—

"According to your faith will it be done to you."
—MATTHEW 9:29

If we desire our faith to be strengthened, we should not retreat from situations where our faith will be tried, for it is through trials that faith is strengthened. In our natural state we dislike dealing with God alone. Through our natural alienation from God, we retreat from Him and from eternal realities, and this tendency remains with us even after regeneration. Consequently, even as believers, to varying degrees we have the same withdrawing from standing with God alone—from depending on Him alone—and yet this is the very position in which we should be if we wish our faith to be strengthened. The more I am in a position for my faith to be tried with reference to my body, my family, my services for the Lord, my business, etc., the more opportunity I will have of seeing God's help and deliverance; and every new instance, in which He helps and delivers me, will tend toward the increase of my faith.

> *The more I am in a position for my faith to be tried… the more opportunity I will have of seeing God's help and deliverance.*

On this account, therefore, the believer should not withdraw from situations, positions, or circumstances in which his faith may be tried. Rather, he should cheerfully embrace them as opportunities where he may see the hand of God stretched out on his behalf to help and deliver him, and whereby he may thus have his faith strengthened.

Only let your trust be *in God,* not *in man,* not *in circumstances,* not *in any of your own efforts,* but real trust in God; and you will be helped in whatever your need may be. You must give up your trust in circumstances, in natural expectations, in former helpers, *but solely rest in God.* This alone will bring the blessing. If we *say* we trust in Him, but in reality do not, then God, taking us at our word, lets us see that we do not really confide in Him; and hence failure arises. On the other hand, if our trust in the Lord is real, help will surely come.

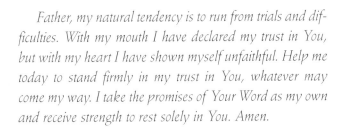

Father, my natural tendency is to run from trials and dif-ficulties. With my mouth I have declared my trust in You, but with my heart I have shown myself unfaithful. Help me today to stand firmly in my trust in You, whatever may come my way. I take the promises of Your Word as my own and receive strength to rest solely in You. Amen.

The Hour of Trial

—❦—

These have come so that your faith—of greater worth than gold, which perishes even though refined by fire—may be proved genuine and may result in praise, glory and honor when Jesus Christ is revealed.
—1 PETER 1:7

An important point for the strengthening of our faith is that we let God work for us when the hour for the trial of our faith comes, and do not work a deliverance of our own. Wherever God has given faith, it is given, among other reasons, for the very purpose of being tried. However weak our faith may be, God will try it. But realize that in the same way He leads us on gently, gradually, and patiently, so also with reference to the trial of our faith. At first our faith will be tried very little in comparison with what it may be afterward, for God never lays more upon us than He is willing to enable us to bear. Now when the trial of faith comes, we are naturally inclined to distrust God and to trust rather in ourselves, or in our friends, or in circumstances. We will want to attempt to work a deliverance of our own, somehow or other, rather than simply look to God and wait for His help.

If we work a deliverance of our own, then at the next trial of our faith we shall again be inclined to deliver ourselves.

But if we do not patiently wait for God's help, if we work a deliverance of our own, then at the next trial of our faith we shall again be inclined to deliver ourselves. And with every new instance of this kind, our faith will decrease; while on the contrary, if we were to stand still, in order to see the salvation of God, to see His hand stretched out in our behalf, trusting in Him alone, then our faith would be increased. So it is that with every fresh case in which the hand of God is stretched out to help us in the hour of trial, our faith would be increased yet more. If the believer desires his faith to be strengthened, he must, especially, *give time to God,* who tries his faith in order to prove to His child, in the end, how willing He is to help and deliver him the moment it is good for him.

Almighty God, I know that there is an hour of trial that is going to come upon the whole world to test those who live on the earth, and there are trials that await me before that day. I would hold on to what I have in You today; I will overcome through Your divine power keeping me in the center of Your hand. Amen.

Spiritual Treasures

———

*"For where your treasure is,
there your heart will be also."*
—MATTHEW 6:21

Treasures stored up on earth bring many cares with them; treasures stored up in heaven never give care. Earthly treasures can never give spiritual joy; heavenly treasures bring with them peace and joy in the Holy Spirit even now. Earthly treasures bring no comfort, and when life is over, they are taken from us; heavenly treasures draw forth thanksgiving that we are permitted and counted worthy to serve the Lord with the means that He has pleased to entrust us as stewards, and when we get to heaven we shall find our treasures there.

Often we hear it said when a person dies that he was worth so much. But a person may die worth a million dollars and yet that person may not possess in God's sight a single dollar because *he was not rich toward God.* Another man may fall asleep in Jesus with very little money, yet in God's sight he may possess a vast treasury in heaven.

Does your soul long to be rich toward God, to store up treasures in heaven?

Does your soul long to be rich toward God, to store up treasures in heaven? The world and its desires pass away (1 John 2:17)! Yet a little while and our stewardship will be taken from us. At present we have the opportunity of serving the Lord with our time, our talents, our strength, our gifts, and also with our property; but shortly this opportunity may cease. O how shortly may it cease. Before you read this I will have fallen asleep in Jesus, and tomorrow you may fall asleep. Therefore, while we have the opportunity, let us serve the Lord.

———∞∞∞———

Lord Jesus, I know that the day is coming when I will depart this life. My desire today is that I might fight the good fight of faith, finish the race set before me, and keep my faith intact in You. May my treasure be the crown of righteousness that You award to all those who have longed for Your appearing. Amen.

Earthly Treasures

———

"Do not store up for yourselves treasures on earth, where moth and rust destroy, and where thieves break in and steal. But store up for yourselves treasures in heaven, where moth and rust do not destroy, and where thieves do not break in and steal."
—MATTHEW 6:19–20

It is the Lord Jesus who speaks this as the lawgiver of His people. He who has infinite wisdom and unfathomable love to us, who knows what is for our real welfare and happiness, and who never asks us anything inconsistent with that love that led Him to lay down His life for us. Remember who it is who speaks to us in these verses.

His counsel, His affectionate entreaty, and His commandment is that His disciples, being strangers and pilgrims on earth, should not seek to store up treasures on earth. All that is of the earth, and in any way connected with it, is subject to corruption, to change, to dissolution. There is no reality in anything else but in heavenly things. Yet a little while and your soul shall be required of you, and what profit shall you have if you have carefully sought to increase your earthly possessions? If there were one particle of real benefit to be derived from it, would not He, whose love to us has been proved to the uttermost, have wished that you and

If, in the slightest degree, it could increase our peace and joy in the Holy Spirit, Jesus would have commanded us to store earthly treasures up.

I should have it? If, in the slightest degree, it could increase our peace and joy in the Holy Spirit, Jesus would have commanded us to store earthly treasures up.

Our Lord however does not merely bid us *not* to store up treasures on earth; for if He had said no more, His commandment might be abused, and persons might find in it an encouragement for their extravagant habits, for their love of pleasure, for their habit of spending everything they have *upon themselves*. Instead He adds that we should store up treasures in heaven. There is such a thing as storing up as truly in heaven as there is storing up on earth. Just as a person can put one sum after another into the bank, so truly our money and lives can be given for the Lord's sake in the work of God. He marks it down in the book of remembrance; He considers it as laid up in heaven. What we give is not lost, it is laid up in the bank of heaven where it remains secure for eternity.

Lord Jesus, I believe that You never forget the work and love and all that we give to others in this lifetime. Help me see what is truly eternal, what is worth giving my life and finances to. Help me to see beyond this world. Amen.

The Kingdom of God

*"But seek first his kingdom and his
righteousness, and all these things
will be given to you as well."*
—MATTHEW 6:33

After our Lord pointed His disciples to the birds of the air and lilies of the field, in order that they should be without worry about the necessities of life, He adds that we should never be anxious for the things that the Gentiles seek, for our heavenly Father knows that we need them.

Observe here particularly that we, the children of God, should be different from the nations of the earth, from those who have no Father in heaven, and who therefore make it their great business what they shall eat and drink as well as how they shall be clothed. We, the children of God, should, as in every other respect, be different from the world and prove

Our great business is to seek the kingdom of God.

to the world that we believe we have a Father in heaven who knows we need all these things. The fact that our almighty Father, who is full of infinite love to His children, knows that we need these things should remove all anxiety from our minds.

Our great business is to seek the kingdom of God. If, according to our ability and according to the opportunity that the Lord gives us, we seek to win souls for the Lord Jesus, that appears to me to be seeking the *external prosperity* of the kingdom of God. If we, as members of the body of Christ, seek to benefit our fellow members in the body, helping them on in grace and truth, or caring for them in any way to their edification, that would be seeking the *internal prosperity* of the kingdom of God. And if we seek His righteousness it means that we seek to be more and more like God, to seek to be inwardly conformed to the mind of God.

Are the things of God, the honor of His name, the welfare of His church, the conversion of sinners, and the profit of your own soul, your chief aim? Or does your business, or your family, or your own temporal concerns *primarily* occupy your attention? Remember that the world passes away, but that the things of God endure forever.

Father, so much of my life has been wasted on pursuing and worrying over the things of this world. I seek Your kingdom today. Establish Your work in my life that I may live so as to benefit Your kingdom forever. Amen.

Holy Independence

⸎

*"Now this is eternal life: that they
may know you, the only true God, and
Jesus Christ, whom you have sent."*
—JOHN 17:3

I t is unspeakably blessed to really know God, to
walk in friendship with Him, to be able to speak
to Him about everything, and to roll upon Him all of
one's cares and burdens. In this blessed way I have
now been enabled to walk for forty-four years, and I
cannot describe the joy of holy independence of circumstances, political events, business difficulties,
friends, death, etc.; for as long as we are able to lean
upon God, we have all we can possibly need. And
this blessed, holy independence may be enjoyed by

all the children of God. It is not only the privilege of a very few favored ones, but all, without exception, who are reconciled to God, by faith in the Lord Jesus, and who trust alone in Him for salvation, may enjoy this blessing.

As long as we are able to lean upon God, we have all we can possibly need.

In order, however, to enjoy this happy fellowship and practical friendship of God and His dear Son, we must walk uprightly. We have to carry out the light that we receive from the Word of God; we must practice the truth we know. Erring and failing we may be, but we must be honest and upright in not living in sin, in not going in a course we know to be contrary to the mind of God. Should the latter be the case, we cannot enjoy fellowship with God, nor shall we be able practically to trust Him as our friend, and this will be the greatest hindrance to having our prayers answered, according to that word: "If I had cherished sin in my heart, the Lord would not have listened" (Ps. 66:18).

Though all believers in the Lord Jesus are not called upon to establish orphan houses or schools for poor children and trust in God for the means, yet all believers, according to the will of God concerning them in Christ Jesus, may cast, and ought to cast, all their care upon Him who cares for them, and need not be anxiously concerned about anything else, as is plainly to be seen throughout Scripture (1 Pet. 5:7; Phil. 4:6; Matt. 6:25–34).

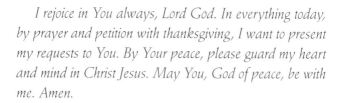

I rejoice in You always, Lord God. In everything today, by prayer and petition with thanksgiving, I want to present my requests to You. By Your peace, please guard my heart and mind in Christ Jesus. May You, God of peace, be with me. Amen.

Work and Prayer

◦────◦

*Then Jesus told his disciples a parable
to show them that they should
always pray and not give up.*
—LUKE 18:1

I t is not enough for the believer to begin to pray,
nor to pray correctly; nor is it enough to continue *for a time* to pray—but we must patiently,
believingly continue in prayer until we obtain an
answer. Further, we have not only *to continue* in
prayer until the end, but we have also *to believe* that
God does hear us and will answer our prayers.
Most frequently we fail *in not continuing* in prayer
until the blessing is obtained, and *in not expecting* the
blessing.

Those who are disciples of the Lord Jesus should labor with all their might in the work of God as if everything depended upon their own endeavors. Yet, having done so, they should not in the least trust in their labor and efforts, nor in the means that they use for the spread of the truth, but in God alone; and they should with all earnestness seek the blessing of God in persevering, patient, and believing prayer.

Most frequently we fail in not continuing in prayer until the blessing is obtained, and in not expecting the blessing.

Here is the great secret of success, my Christian reader. Work with all your might, but never trust in your work. Pray with all your might for the blessing in God, but work at the same time with all diligence, with all patience, with all perseverance. Pray, then, and work. Work and pray. And still again pray, and then work. And so on, all the days of your life. The result will surely be abundant blessing. Whether you *see* much fruit or little fruit, such kind of service will be blessed.

Lord Jesus, I ask Your blessing on everything I do today. I will serve You with all my heart, but I know how foolish it is to trust in my own efforts. If Your Holy Spirit does not breathe life into these labors, they remain dead and fruitless. Breathe on them, Spirit of God, and may Jesus be lifted up today for others to see. Amen.

Heart Reality

*Love must be sincere. Hate what is evil; cling to
what is good. Be devoted to one another in brotherly love.
Honor one another above yourselves. Never be lacking in zeal,
but keep your spiritual fervor, serving the Lord. Be joyful in
hope, patient in affliction, faithful in prayer.*
—ROMANS 12:9–12

No one ever knew Jehovah without being able
to exercise faith in Him. It is when God is not
known that difficulty comes. The great point therefore is to acquaint ourselves with God, to know God
for ourselves as He has revealed Himself in the
Scriptures.

Our holy faith does not consist in *talking.* "Reality,
reality, reality" is what we want. Let us have *heart-work;* let us be genuine. We should love so as to be

missed—missed both in the Church and in the world—when we are removed! Oh how rapidly is time hastening on! We should live in such a manner as that, if we are called hence, our dear brothers and sisters might feel our loss, and from their inmost souls exclaim, "Oh that such a one were in our midst again!" We should be missed even by the world. Worldly people should be constrained to say of us, "If ever there was a Christian upon earth, that man was one."

The living God is with us, whose power never fails, whose arm never grows weary, whose wisdom is infinite.

The living God is with us, whose power never fails, whose arm never grows weary, whose wisdom is infinite, and whose power is unchanging. Therefore today, tomorrow, and next month, as long as life is continued, He will be our helper and friend. Still more, even as He is through all time, so will He be through all eternity.

Heavenly Father, reality in my spiritual life is what I want. My heart's only desire is to know You for who You are, to worship You alone, and to love You alone. Words can be spoken so easily, but You know my heart. Help me to live my life in such a way that the world is different because I've been here. Your arm has not grown weary, Lord. Extend Your touch into my spirit today and make me an instrument for Your peace. Amen.

Love and Prayer

—⟨⟨⟨⟨⟩⟩⟩⟩—

*"Ask and it will be given to you; seek and you
will find; knock and the door will be opened to you.
For everyone who asks receives; he who seeks finds;
and to him who knocks, the door will be opened."*
—MATTHEW 7:7–8

Our heavenly Father loves all His children with infinite love; that is, He loves everyone, even the weakest of His children with the same love that He loves His only begotten Son. On account of this infinite love—knowing how great, how varied, how numberless would be their trials, their difficulties, their afflictions, their temptations, while passing through this vale of tears—He, in His grace, made abundant provision for them in giving most precious and encouraging promises concerning prayer.

If they would take their trials and difficulties to their heavenly Father, seeking His strength, His counsel, and His guidance, and acting according to the loving counsel and advice given in the Scriptures—"Cast all your anxiety on him because he cares for you" (1 Pet. 5:7)—the position of most of the children of God would be very different from what it is.

The Father loves His children with the same love that He loves His only begotten Son.

Then again, our precious Lord Jesus Christ loves us with the same love that the Father loves Him. Do we believe it? It may seem strange to some people that the Father loves His children with the same love that He loves His only begotten Son, and that the Lord Jesus Christ loves us with that same love—and that with this love He loves the feeblest and weakest of His children. Yet this is the clear statement of John 15:9 and 17:23. Our precious Lord Jesus, who loves us with such love, passed through difficulties, trials, and temptations, like unto ours, while He was in this world. He was looked down upon; He was despised; that Blessed One had nowhere to lay His head and was, while in this world tempted at every point as we are, yet was without sin.

Knowing the position of His disciples in this world, He has given the precious promise that we may have Him as the burden-bearer, ever ready to help in time of sorrow, weakness, and affliction—in all the variety of positions and circumstances in which we are found here in the body.

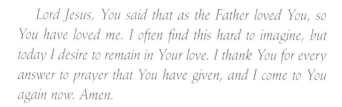

Lord Jesus, You said that as the Father loved You, so You have loved me. I often find this hard to imagine, but today I desire to remain in Your love. I thank You for every answer to prayer that You have given, and I come to You again now. Amen.

Spiritual Illumination

⇛

*We have not received the spirit of the world
but the Spirit who is from God, that we may
understand what God has freely given us.*
—1 CORINTHIANS 2:12

Does anyone ask me what I think is the best way of reading the Scriptures? In the first place, in order to have a deeper acquaintance with the Scriptures, it is absolutely needful that you regularly read the entire Bible through—not as some do, taking the Bible and reading wherever it opens. If it opens on Psalm 103, they read it, if at John 14 or Romans 8, they read those portions of Scripture. Let me lovingly say that it is wrong for a child of God to so treat the Father's Book; it is wrong for the disciple of the Lord Jesus to so treat his blessed Master. Let me lovingly urge those who have not done so, to begin the Old Testament from the beginning, and the New Testament from the beginning, at one time reading in the Old, and at another time in the New Testament, keeping a mark in their Bible to show how far they have come.

Come again and again to God, and He will guide you little by little, and further instruct you in the knowledge of His will.

Why is it important to do this? There is a special purpose in the arrangement of the Scriptures. They begin with the creation of the world and close with the end of the world. Just as you read a biography or history book, commencing at the beginning and reading through to the end, so should you read the revelation of God's will, and when you get to the end, begin again and again.

But this is not all that is necessary. When you come to this blessed Book, the great point is to come with a deep consciousness of your ignorance, seeking on your knees the help of God, that by His Spirit

He may graciously instruct you. If you do not understand some portions, do not be discouraged, but come again and again to God, and He will guide you little by little, and further instruct you in the knowledge of His will. And with an increasing knowledge of God obtained in a prayerful, humble way, you will receive, not something that simply fills the head, but something that exercises the heart, and cheers, and comforts, and strengthens your inner man.

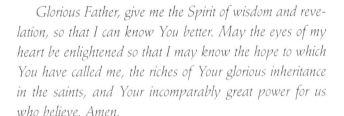

Glorious Father, give me the Spirit of wisdom and revelation, so that I can know You better. May the eyes of my heart be enlightened so that I may know the hope to which You have called me, the riches of Your glorious inheritance in the saints, and Your incomparably great power for us who believe. Amen.

A Prayer Record

*"This is what the L*ORD *says,*
*he who made the earth, the L*ORD *who*
*formed it and established it—the L*ORD *is his name:*
'Call to me and I will answer you and tell you great
and unsearchable things you do not know.'"
—JEREMIAH 33:2–3

I have found it a great blessing to treasure up in my memory the answers God graciously gives me to prayer. I have always kept a written record to strengthen the memory. I advise the keeping of a little memorandum book. On one side—say to the left hand side—put down the request, and the date when you began to offer it. Let the opposite page be left blank to put down the answer in each case, and you will soon find how many answers you get, and thus you will be encouraged more and more, and your faith will be strengthened. You will see what a lovely, bountiful, and gracious Being God is; your heart will go out more and more in love to God, and you will say, "It is my heavenly Father who has been so kind. I will trust in Him. I will confide in Him."

You will soon find how many answers you get, and thus you will be encouraged more and more, and your faith will be strengthened.

Behold, esteemed reader, the goodness of God! Behold also the recompense that, sooner or later, the Lord gives to His children, who wait upon Him and trust in Him! Often it may appear that we wait upon the Lord in vain, but in His own time, God will abundantly prove that it was not in vain. Continue to make known your requests to Him, but do also expect help from Him. You honor God by believing that He does hear your prayers, and that He will answer them.

———∞∞∞———

Who among the gods is like You, O Lord? Who is like You—majestic in holiness, awesome in glory, working wonders? You stretch out Your right hand and answer our prayers. In Your unfailing love You will lead the people whom You have redeemed. May You reign forever and ever. Amen.

Spiritual Nourishment

∽∾∽

I rejoice in following your statutes as one
rejoices in great riches. I meditate on your precepts
and consider your ways. I delight in your decrees;
I will not neglect your word.
—PSALM 119:14–16

I have made it my habit to begin every day by reading and meditating on the Word of God. The result I have found to be almost invariably this, that very soon my soul has been led to confession, or to thanksgiving, or to intercession, or to supplication—so that, though I did not, as it were, give myself to *prayer,* but to *meditation,* yet my meditation turned almost immediately more or less into prayer. Then after I have been making confession, or intercession, or supplication, or have given thanks for a while, I go on to the next word or verse, turning all the knowledge into prayer for myself and others, as the word may lead to it, but still continually keeping before me the fact that the object of my meditation is food for my own soul.

The result of this is that there is always a good deal of confession, thanksgiving, supplication, or intercession mingled with my meditation; and that my inner man almost invariably is consciously nourished and strengthened; and that by breakfast time, with rare exceptions, I am in a peaceful, if not happy, state of heart. This has also been a way by which the Lord is pleased to communicate to me that which, either very soon after or at a later time, I have found to become food for other believers, though it was not for the sake of the public ministry of the Word that I gave myself to meditation, but for the profit of my inner man.... I dwell so particularly on this point because of the immense

Though I did not, as it were, give myself to prayer, but to meditation, yet my meditation turned almost immediately more or less into prayer.

spiritual profit and refreshment I am conscious of having derived from it myself, and I affectionately and solemnly beseech all my fellow believers to ponder this matter.

Heavenly Father, open my eyes that I may see wonderful things in Your law. My soul is consumed with longing for Your laws at all times. Let me understand the teaching of Your precepts; then I will meditate on Your wonders. Amen.

Spiritual Priorities

Jesus answered, "It is written: 'Man does not live on bread alone, but on every word that comes from the mouth of God.'"
—MATTHEW 4:4

The very first and primary business to which I ought to attend every day is to have my soul happy in the Lord. The first thing to be concerned about is not how much I can serve the Lord, nor how I might glorify the Lord, but how I might get my soul into a happy state and how my inner man might be nourished. For I might seek to set the truth before unbelievers, I might seek to benefit other believers, I might seek to help the poor, I might in other ways seek to live my life as an exemplary child of God in this world, and yet, not being happy in the Lord and not being nourished and strengthened in my inner man day by day, all this might not be attended to in a right spirit.

> *The most important thing I have to do is to give myself first to reading the Word of God and to meditation on it.*

My practice in years past was to give myself to prayer after getting dressed in the morning. Now I see that the most important thing I have to do is to give myself first to reading the Word of God and to meditation on it—that my heart might be comforted, encouraged, warned, reproved, instructed, and that by means of the Word of God, while meditating on it, my heart might be brought into experiential communion with the Lord. I began, therefore, immediately after rising early in the morning, to meditate on the New Testament. The first thing I do, after having asked in a few words the Lord's blessing upon His precious Word, is to begin to meditate on the Word of God, searching as it were into every verse to get a blessing out of it, not for the sake of the public

ministry of the Word, not for the sake of preaching
on what I had meditated upon, but for the sake of
obtaining good for my own soul.

*Holy Spirit, fill my mind and heart with Your thoughts
as I come to receive from Your Word. Strengthen my inner
man, illuminate my soul, that I might see and know the truth
in all its power. Let these precious words come to life within
me and cause my soul to be blessed and filled with joy.
Amen.*

True Worship

∝∞∝

Therefore, I urge you, brothers, in view of God's mercy,
to offer your bodies as living sacrifices, holy and pleasing
to God—this is your spiritual act of worship.
—ROMANS 12:1

All Christians do not look on trials, afflictions, losses, pain, sickness, bereavement, as a dispensation intended by God for their good; and yet these difficulties are invariably intended for the believer's good. We should seek continually to recognize the hand of God in all His dealings with us, and believe that all are intended for our real profit. "And we know that in all things God works for the good of those who love him, who have been called according to his purpose" (Rom. 8:28).

I would especially advise my fellow believers in the Lord Jesus to seek more and more to enter into the grace and love of God in giving His only begotten Son, and into the grace and love of the Lord Jesus in giving Himself in our place, in order that, constrained by love and gratitude, they may be increasingly led to surrender their physical and mental strength, their time, gifts, talents, property, position in life, rank, and all they have and are to the Lord. By this I do not mean that they should give up their business, trade, or profession and become preachers; nor do I mean that they should take all their money and give it to the first beggar who asks for it, but that they should hold all they have and are for the Lord, not as owners, but as stewards, and be willing, at His bidding, to use for Him part or all that they have. However short the believer may fall, nothing less than this should be his aim.

Seek more and more to enter into the grace and love of God in giving His only begotten Son, and into the grace and love of the Lord Jesus in giving Himself in our place.

It is so easy, Lord Jesus, to not lay everything in our lives at Your feet. It is so easy to not believe that You are working in all the circumstances of my life to shape Your image in my heart. Open my eyes to see what You have done for me; break my heart that I might be able to give You all of my heart. Amen.

Spiritual Direction

⎯⎯⎯∞⎯⎯⎯

The path of the righteous is like the first gleam
of dawn, shining ever brighter till the full light of day.
But the way of the wicked is like deep darkness;
they do not know what makes them stumble.
—PROVERBS 4:18–19

To know the Lord's will we should use biblical means. Prayer, the Word of God, and His Spirit should be united together. We should go to the Lord repeatedly in prayer and ask Him to teach us by His Spirit through His Word. I say by His Spirit through His Word for if we should think that His Spirit led us to do so and so, because certain facts are so and so, and yet His Word is opposed to the step that we are going to take, we should be deceiving ourselves. No situation, no business will be given to me *by God*, in which I have not time enough to care about my soul. Therefore, however outward circumstances may appear, it can only be considered as permitted of God to prove the genuineness of my love, faith, and obedience, but by no means as the leading of His providence to induce me to act contrary to His revealed will.

> *No situation, no business will be given to me by God, in which I have not time enough to care about my soul.*

Prayer and faith, the universal remedies against every need and every difficulty, and the nourishment of prayer and faith through God's holy Word, have helped me over all the difficulties. I never remember, in all my Christian course, a period now of sixty-nine years, that I ever *sincerely* and *patiently* sought to know the will of God by the *teaching of the Holy Spirit* through the instrumentality of the *Word of God,* but I have been *always* directed rightly. But if *honesty of heart* and *uprightness before God* were lacking, or if I did not *patiently* wait upon God for instruction, or if I preferred the *counsel of my fellow men* to the declarations of the *Word of the living God,* I made great mistakes.

———⊰⊱———

Heavenly Father, I want to hear what You are saying to me. I want to listen closely to Your words. I will not let them out of my sight, and I will keep them within my heart, for they are life to me and health to my whole body. By faith and prayer I will guard my heart. Lead me in Your ways. Amen.

Living in the Will of God

‒‒◦◦◦‒‒

*Be very careful, then, how you live—not as
unwise but as wise, making the most of every
opportunity, because the days are evil. Therefore do not
be foolish, but understand what the Lord's will is.*
—EPHESIANS 5:15–17

How important it is to discover the will of God
before we undertake anything, because we are
then not only blessed in our own souls, but also the
work of our hands will prosper. For in as many
points as we are acting according to the mind of
God, so in those are we blessed and made a blessing.
Our manner of living is according to the mind of the
Lord, for He delights in seeing His children thus

come to Him (Matt. 6); and therefore, though I am weak and erring in many points, yet He blesses me in these particulars.

This is the counsel I give to believers who ask me about the will of God. (1) Be slow to take new steps in the Lord's service, or in your business, or in your families. Weigh everything well; weigh all in the light of the Word of God and in the fear of God. (2) Seek to have no will of your own, in order to discover the mind of God, regarding any steps you propose to take, so that you can honestly say, you are willing to do the will of God,

When you have found out what the will of God is, seek for His help.

if He will only be pleased to instruct you. (3) But when you have found out what the will of God is, seek for His help. Seek it sincerely, perseveringly, patiently, believingly, and expectantly; and you will surely, in His own time and way, obtain it.

We do not have to rush forward in self-will and say, I will do the work, and I will trust the Lord for means. This cannot be real trust. It is the counterfeit of faith; it is presumption, although God, in great pity and mercy, may even help us finally. Yet accomplishing it does not prove that we were right in going forward before His time was come. We should, rather, under such circumstances say to ourselves: Am I indeed doing *the work of God?* And if so, *I* may not be the person to do it; or if I am the person, *His time* may not yet have come for me to go forward. It may be His good pleasure to exercise my faith and patience. I ought, therefore, quietly to wait His time; for when it is come, God will help. Acting on this principle brings blessing.

Holy Spirit, fill my life that I might know the will of the Father in everything I do. Give me wisdom so that the decisions I make will be fruitful for the kingdom of God. Shine Your light upon the path I am to walk with my life. Amen.

Pure Spiritual Milk

———— ✺ ————

*Therefore, rid yourselves of all malice
and deceit, hypocrisy, envy, and slander of every
kind. Like newborn babies, crave pure spiritual milk,
so that by it you may grow up in your salvation, now
that you have tasted that the Lord is good.*
—1 PETER 2:1–3

O ne of the most deeply important points is that of attending to the careful, prayerful reading of the Word of God, and meditation in it. As growth in the natural life is attained by proper food, so in the spiritual life; if we desire to grow, this growth is only attained through the instrumentality of the Word of God. The apostle Peter does not state, as some might be very willing to say, that "The reading of the Word may be of importance under some circumstances."

Nor is it stated that you may gain profit by reading the statements that I will make; it is of the Word, and of the Word alone, that the apostle speaks, and nothing else.

There is such a thing as babies being neglected, and what is the consequence?

They never become healthy men or women, because of that early neglect.

You may say that the reading of a certain book often does you good. I do not question it. Nevertheless, the instrumentality of God has been pleased to appoint and to use is that of *the Word itself;* and just in the measure in which the disciples of the Lord Jesus attend to this, they will be strong in the Lord; and in so far as it is neglected, so far will they be weak. There is such a thing as babies being neglected, and what is the consequence? They never become healthy men or women, because of that early neglect.

Perhaps—and it is one of the most hurtful forms of this neglect—they obtain improper food, and therefore do not attain the full vigor of maturity. So with regard to the divine life. It is a deeply important point, that we obtain right spiritual food at the very beginning of that life. What is that food? It is the "pure spiritual milk" of the Word of God. That is the only proper nourishment for the strengthening of the new life.

———✺———

Holy Spirit, thank you for giving me the Word of God to sustain my spiritual life. All Scripture is God-breathed and is profitable for teaching, rebuking, and correcting and training me in righteousness, that I might be thoroughly equipped for every good work. There is never a moment when I can get by without the strength I receive from the pure spiritual milk of Your Word. Help me to take it into my heart today. Amen.

More Grace

⁕

For he chose us in him before the creation
of the world to be holy and blameless in his sight.
In love he predestined us to be adopted as his sons
through Jesus Christ, in accordance with his pleasure
and will—to the praise of his glorious grace, which
he has freely given us in the One he loves.
—EPHESIANS 1:4–6

I am happier now, after being a believer nearly
fifty-one years, than I was fifty years ago; happier far than I was forty years ago, than I was thirty
years ago, than I was twenty years ago, than I was
ten years ago. As the time has gone on, my peace
and joy and happiness in the Lord have increased
more and more, instead of declining more and more.

Why do I refer to this? Not to boast, for it is all by the grace of God, but to encourage my younger fellow believers to expect greater things from the Lord, who delights in giving abundantly. And as you sing sometimes, "More and more, more and more," there is yet more to come. Let us look out for it, for God delights to give more grace. It is the joy and delight of His heart to give more and more.

Expect greater things from the Lord, who delights in giving abundantly.… It is the joy and delight of His heart to give more and more.

Why should it not be? Why should we not have the best things in the last part of life? Has God changed? Far from it! Is the Bible changed? No! We have the same blessed Word. Is the power of the Holy Spirit less? Far different from that; nothing of the kind! The Lord Jesus Christ is ever ready to bless. The Word we now have is the whole revelation. And our heavenly Father has the same heart toward His children. Therefore there is nothing to hinder our being happier as time goes with us.

Jesus, our redemption is through Your blood, the forgiveness of our sins. It is the riches of Your grace that have been lavished upon us with all wisdom and understanding. Praise to our God and Father who has blessed us in the heavenly realms with every spiritual blessing found in You. Amen.

Expectancy in Prayer

———— ✺ ————

*I write these things to you who believe in the name
of the Son of God so that you may know that you have
eternal life. This is the confidence we have in approaching
God: that if we ask anything according to his will, he hears us.
And if we know that he hears us—whatever we ask—we
know that we have what we asked of him.*
—1 JOHN 5:13–15

Here then is the first point to be noticed with regard to prayer. If we desire to have our petitions granted, we must first see to it that we ask for things according to God's mind and will, for our blessing and happiness are intimately connected with the holiness of God.

Suppose there was a person known to be lazy and idle who hears the promises about prayer. What if he said, "I will try these promises, and I will ask God to give me one million dollars, and then I can sit back and enjoy myself"? If he prays in this manner every day, will he obtain it? Assuredly not! Why not? He does not ask for it that he might use it for the work of God, but he asks that he may spend it on himself. He is not asking according to the mind of God, and therefore however long or sincerely he may pray, he will not get the answer. We can only expect our prayers to be answered when we ask according to the mind of God.

Just as by faith in the Lord Jesus we shall stand before God at the last day, so it is now in approaching God in prayer.

The second point we should notice is that we do not ask on account of our own goodness or merit, but in the name of the Lord Jesus Christ (John 14:13–14). Just as by faith in the Lord Jesus we shall stand before God at the last day, so it is now in approaching God in prayer. If we desire to have our prayers answered, we must come to Him as sinners who trust in Jesus, who by faith are united to the blessed risen Lord, who have become, through trusting in Him, members of that body of which He is the head.

Let none suppose they are good enough in themselves. I deserve nothing but hell. For fifty-four years, by God's grace, I have walked in the fear of God, and by His grace have lived such a life that no one can point to me and say I am a hypocrite. Yet if I had what I deserve, I would expect nothing but hell. I deserve nothing but hell. So precisely with all of you, and the very best and holiest persons that can be found.

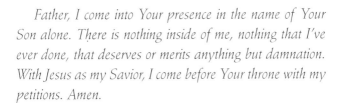

Father, I come into Your presence in the name of Your Son alone. There is nothing inside of me, nothing that I've ever done, that deserves or merits anything but damnation. With Jesus as my Savior, I come before Your throne with my petitions. Amen.

Conditions for Answered Prayer

"But the tax collector stood at a distance. He would not even look up to heaven, but beat his breast and said, 'God, have mercy on me, a sinner.'"
—LUKE 18:13

On the ground of our own goodness we cannot expect to have our prayers answered. But Jesus is worthy, and for His sake we may have our prayers answered. There is nothing too choice, too costly, or too great for God to give Him. He is worthy. He is the spotless, holy Child, who under all circumstances acted according to the mind of God. And if we trust in Him, if we hide in Him, if we put Him forward and ourselves in the background, depend on

Him and plead His name, we may expect to have our prayers answered.

Someone says, "I have prayed through long years for my unconverted children, but I am so unworthy that my prayers will be unanswered." This is a mistake. The promises are particularly for such—for the weak, for the feeblest, for the ignorant, for the needy; and all such who ask for Christ's sake are warranted to expect their prayers to be answered.

The promises are particularly for…the weak, for the feeblest, for the ignorant, for the needy.

But if it means, "I live in sin," the prayer cannot be answered, for we read, "If I had cherished sin in my heart, the Lord would not have listened" (Ps. 66:18). If I live in sin, and go on in a course hateful to God, I may not expect my prayers to be answered.

A third condition is that we exercise faith in the power and willingness of God to answer our prayers. This is deeply important. "Whatever you ask for in prayer, believe that you have received it, and it will be yours" (Mark 11:24).

I have found invariably, in the fifty-four years during which I have been a believer, that if I only believed, I was sure to get, in God's time, the thing I asked for. I would especially lay this on your heart that you exercise faith in the power and willingness of God to answer your requests. To see that He has almighty power, you only need to look at the resurrection of the Lord Jesus Christ from the dead. As to the love of God, you have only to look to the cross of Christ and see His love in not sparing His Son from death. With these proofs of the power and love of God, assuredly, if we believe, we shall receive—we shall obtain.

⸻

Father, I know what the tax collector felt when he beat his chest. I come to You because Jesus has made a way through His atoning blood and the power of His resurrection. I bring my requests believing that You hear me and are willing to answer. Amen.

Heart Knowledge of God

‱

I want to know Christ and the power of his resurrection and the fellowship of sharing in his sufferings, becoming like him in his death.
—PHILIPPIANS 3:10

One cannot stress enough the importance of our hearts practically entering into the loveliness of the nature and character of God. We have therefore to seek for ourselves to become more and more convinced of the graciousness of God, of His love, His bountifulness, His kindness, His pity, His compassion, His readiness to help and bless, His patience, His faithfulness, His almighty power, His infinite wisdom; in a word, we have to seek to know God, not according to the view of men, but according to the revelation He has made of Himself in the Holy Scriptures.

The heart knowledge of God tends to holiness: The more I know of God, the more I am constrained to admire Him, and to say, "What a lovely, good being He is!" and especially when I see His wondrous love in Christ Jesus to such a guilty, wicked creature as I am. Therefore my heart is constrained to seek to imitate God, to seek to do something in return for His love, and to be more like God Himself.

What will make us so exceedingly happy in heaven? It will be the fuller knowledge of God.

The heart knowledge of God also tends to happiness: The more we know of God, the happier we are. It was when we were in entire ignorance of God that we were without real peace or joy. When we became a little acquainted with God, our peace and joy—our true happiness, I mean—commenced; and the more we become acquainted with Him, the more truly happy we become. What will make us so exceedingly happy in heaven? It will be the fuller knowledge of God—we shall know Him far better than we now do.

The heart knowledge of God also tends to our usefulness in His service here: It is impossible that I can enter into what God has done for sinners without being constrained in return to seek to live for Him, to labor for Him. I ask myself, "What can I do for Him who has bestowed upon me His choicest gifts?" Hence I am constrained to labor for Him. According to the measure in which I am fully acquainted with God, do I seek to labor for Him. I cannot be idle.

Father, what a privilege it is to know You, and to be Your child. To know You is eternal life. To know Your love surpasses knowledge. Purify my heart that I might know You more and more. Amen.

Leanness of Soul

⸺◈⸺

[They] lusted exceedingly in the wilderness,
and tempted God in the desert. And he gave them
their request; but sent leanness into their soul.
—PSALM 106:14–15 KJV

How unfortunate it is that so many of God's children do not truly desire that all they have should be the Lord's, if He should call for it. They have not reached even so far as Jacob had, who did not live in the light of this present dispensation, but who, at the first dawning of spiritual light, said to God, "Of all that you give me I will give you a tenth" (Gen. 28:22). They do not give back to the Lord the tenth part of all He is pleased to give them.

They willingly lay out the finances for the purchase of a house and the education of their children, hire much of their work done for them, and spend money on luxuries, and yet spend proportionally little for the work of God, for the support of poor saints, or in feeding hungry people near them, who cannot earn their living. But as they live more for themselves, or for their children, than for God, so they are not really happy in God, which is one of the blessings that God meant for them to enjoy during their earthly existence. But this has not only to do with the rich or the middle classes of the children of God, but even with the poorer classes. The Christian man with a small income says, "I have so little, I cannot spare anything; or, if something, it can only be the smallest amount."

They live more for themselves, or for their children, than for God, so they are not really happy in God.

And what is the result? Either all, or almost all, finances are spent upon himself, or that which is not needed is put away for future days. The consequence is that such individuals are not happy spiritually, and they often do not prosper temporally, because as they are not faithful over the little with which God is pleased to entrust them, He cannot entrust them with more. As God did to Israel, He may be gracious to send chastisement and leanness into their soul, or to lead them to see the vanity of such things. Often also, in the case of the poorer, the middle, or the richer classes, God is obliged to send sickness or heavy losses in order that He may take from His children what they would not gladly, constrained by the love of Christ, lay down at His feet.

I give thanks to You, O Lord, for You are good, and Your love endures forever. My desire is to constantly do what is right in Your eyes. Show me Your favor that I may share in the joy of Your nation and join your inheritance in giving thanks. Amen.

Constrained by the Love of Christ

—∞∞∞—

Each man should give what he has decided in his heart to give, not reluctantly or under compulsion, for God loves a cheerful giver. And God is able to make all grace abound to you, so that in all things at all times, having all that you need, you will abound in every good work.
—2 CORINTHIANS 9:7–8

I am often asked how a believer should live in order to best use his finances for the Lord. Seek first to remember that the Lord Jesus Christ has redeemed you, and that you are not your own, because you are "bought at a price" (1 Cor. 6:20), even "the precious blood of Christ, a lamb without blemish or defect" (1 Pet. 1:19). All that we have and are belongs to Him, and we take the position with our possessions as a faithful steward would who is entrusted with goods or money by a rich proprietor.

We take the position with our possessions as a faithful steward would who is entrusted with goods or money by a rich proprietor.

The regular use of our means as the Lord prospers us is the next thing to be attended to. As far as practicable, we should seek to do this *weekly,* according to the word, "On the first day of every week, each one of you should set aside a sum of money in keeping with his income" (1 Cor. 16:2). I sincerely say that this point should be considered by Christians in the fear of God. *It is God's principle, most plainly laid down in God's Word.* But if, through particular circumstances, this weekly and proportionate giving is impracticable, then the first time we are able to ascertain how our business stands, how much our profession has brought us in, etc., we should settle before God how much, accordingly, we can give for the work of God or for the poor.

It is to be noticed, also, that the injunction of the Holy Spirit, through the apostle Paul, is not only that one or another should do so, but that *everyone* should do so—the rich, those of the middle classes, and even those of the poorer classes.

With regard to *the amount* to be given, no rule can be laid down, because what we do should be done not in a legal spirit, but from love and gratitude to that Blessed One who died for us. God desires us to act in the spirit of sonship and as constrained by the love of Christ to us. For those whom He has made His children, His heirs and joint heirs with Christ, He therefore give no commandment with regard to this point.

Lord Jesus, free my heart from a spirit of legalism. May everything I give, my service and my finances, reflect the joy of being Your child. All that I am and have is Yours. Amen.

Joyful Giving

———— ✹ ————

One man gives freely, yet gains even more; another withholds unduly, but comes to poverty. A generous man will prosper; he who refreshes others will himself be refreshed.
—PROVERBS 11:24–25

Over the past forty years in the service of the Lord, I have become acquainted with many thousands of believers. Many, very many, have honored me with desiring my counsel and advice in their private affairs. From these many instances I have seen the truth of how one gives freely, and yet gains more. But far more have I seen in which they withheld unduly, but it only tended to poverty.

Notice the words, "another withholds unduly." It is not said that he withholds all, but "unduly"—

while he gives, it is so little, in comparison with what it might be, and should be, that it comes to poverty. With all the desire to get on with their finances, many people are not able to do so because they only live for themselves. Bad debts, unexpected and unaccountable loss of business, heavy family afflictions, etc., take away the money that they seek to keep for themselves, contrary to the will of God. While, on the other hand, I know many believers who, from giving ten percent at first, have increased to fifteen and twenty percent, and I know of some who give sixty and seventy-five percent of

> *With all the desire to get on with their finances, many people are not able to do so because they only live for themselves.*

their whole income, because they desire to be "rich toward God" and not to store "up things for himself" (Luke 12:21).

Though we should never give *for the sake of being repaid by the Lord,* still, this will be the case, *if we give from right motives.* It is God's own declaration that it will be so. This is plainly to be gathered from the following passages: "Honor the LORD with your wealth, with the firstfruits of all your crops; then your barns will be filled to overflowing, and your vats will brim over with new wine" (Prov. 3:9–10). "Give, and it will be given to you. A good measure, pressed down, shaken together and running over, will be poured into your lap" (Luke 6:38). "He who is kind to the poor lends to the LORD, and he will reward him for what he has done" (Prov. 19:17).

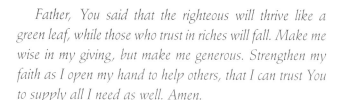

Father, You said that the righteous will thrive like a green leaf, while those who trust in riches will fall. Make me wise in my giving, but make me generous. Strengthen my faith as I open my hand to help others, that I can trust You to supply all I need as well. Amen.

Good Stewards

*"Bring the whole tithe into the storehouse.... Test me
in this," says the* LORD *Almighty, "and see if I will not
throw open the floodgates of heaven and pour out so much
blessing that you will not have room enough for it."*
—MALACHI 3:10

At the end of the nineteenth century a very godly
and generous merchant in London was called
on by a gentleman to ask him for money for a char-
itable project. The gentleman expected very little,
having just heard that the merchant had sustained
heavy loss from the wreck of some of his ships.
Contrary, however, to expectation, he received about
ten times as much as he had expected for his project.
He was unable to refrain from expressing his sur-
prise to the merchant, describing what he had heard

and how he doubted the merchant would give much of anything, and he asked whether he was mistaken about the shipwreck of the vessels. The merchant replied, "It was quite true, I have sustained heavy loss by these vessels being wrecked. But that is the very reason why I give so much, for I must make better use of my stewardship, before it is entirely taken from me."

> *How should we respond if prosperity in our business… should suddenly cease, notwithstanding our having given a considerable portion of our means to the Lord's work?*

How should we respond if prosperity in our business, our trade, our profession, etc., should suddenly cease, notwithstanding our having given a considerable portion of our means to the Lord's work? Solomon's reply would have been, "When times are bad, consider" (Eccl. 7:14). It is the will of God that we should consider our ways, that we should see whether there is any particular reason why God has allowed this to happen to us. We may discover that we have taken our prosperity too much as a matter of course rather than having recognized *practically* the hand of God in our success. Or it may be that while the Lord has prospered us that we have spent too much on ourselves, and we may have, though unintentionally, *abused* the blessing of God. I do not mean by this remark to bring any children of God into the bondage of a scrupulous conscience that worries over every penny. Yet, there is truly such a thing as propriety or impropriety in our dress, our furniture, our table, our house, our lifestyle, and in the yearly amount we spend on ourselves and family.

———— ✦ ————

Lord Almighty, I dread that it might be said of my life that I robbed You by refusing to give of my life and means. I desire to give freely and abundantly that Your name may be exalted among the nations. Amen.

Patience

———∞———

*I waited patiently for the LORD; he turned to me
and heard my cry. He lifted me out of the slimy pit,
out of the mud and mire; he set my feet on a rock and
gave me a firm place to stand. He put a new song in
my mouth, a hymn of praise to our God.*
—PSALM 40:1–3

Someone may ask, "Is it necessary that I should bring a matter before God two, three, five, or even twenty times? Is it not enough I tell Him once?" We might as well say there is no need to tell Him once, for He knows beforehand what our needs are. He wants us to prove that we have confidence, that we take our place as creatures toward the Creator.

Moreover we are never to lose sight of the fact that there may be particular reasons why prayer may not at once be answered. One reason may be the need for the exercise of our faith, for by exercise faith is strengthened. We all know that if our faith is not exercised it remains as it was at first. By the trial it is strengthened. Another reason may be that we may glorify God by the manifestation of patience. This is a grace by which God is greatly magnified. Our manifestation of patience glorifies God. There may be another reason. Our heart may not yet be prepared for the answer to our prayer.

When the heart is prepared for the blessing, it will be given by God.

Many of the dear children of God stagger, because prayer is not at once answered. And because for weeks, months, and years prayer remains unanswered, they cease to ask God, and thus they lose the blessing that, had they persevered, they would assuredly have obtained. When the heart is prepared for the blessing, it will be given by God.

All God's children, who walk in His ways and wait for Him in prayer, have some prayers that are answered quickly and others for which they wait long for an answer. Often, before leaving my bed-room in the morning, I already have had a prayer answered. But sometimes I have had to wait weeks, months, years, sometimes many years. But I hope in God, I pray on and look yet for the answers.

Go on waiting upon God, go on praying; only be sure you ask for things that are according to the mind of God. Go on praying; expect an answer, look for it, and in the end you will have the opportunity to praise God for it.

<hr>

O Lord my God, many are the wonders You have done. I wait patiently for You. In Your own time and in Your own way, You will answer even my most difficult prayers. Help me to not stagger in unbelief. Amen.